MARY BEA SULL

D0106325

Living

THE
Way of Love

A 40-DAY DEVOTIONAL
Foreword by Courtney V. Cowart & Stephanie Spellers

**CHURCH
PUBLISHING
INCORPORATED**

To Malcolm, Brendan, Kiki, and Marcy—
wherever you go, I send a piece of my heart with you.
You are my primary teachers in the way of love.

Church Publishing
19 East 34th Street
New York, NY 10016
www.churchpublishing.org

Cover design by Beth Oberholtzer
Author photo: Alice Thigpen
Layout and typesetting by Beth Oberholtzer

A record of this book is available from the Library of Congress.

ISBN-13: 9781640652309 (pbk.)
ISBN-13: 9781640652316 (ebook)

Printed in the United States of America

Contents

Foreword

In December 2017, Presiding Bishop Michael Curry invited twelve leaders to pray with him about how Episcopalians could place Jesus at the center of our lives and embrace evangelism as an essential part of our faith. In that circle Bishop Curry reminded us that the Jesus Movement is not trying to increase the number of people in our pews or to maintain the institution. It is welcoming people to journey toward a faith and a life saturated in Jesus Christ. It's about worshiping *and* following Jesus; small communities who intentionally follow Jesus will find their own lives changed and thus be catalysts for changing the world.

As two of the twelve gathered with Bishop Curry, we were captivated by his vision for living out the Jesus Movement. But how? What are the conditions under which people of faith—or no faith at all—can shift from going to church to owning and sharing a loving, liberating, life-giving relationship with God in Christ? We knew it had to start with small communities of Christians engaging in the most basic and time-tested practices.

We dreamt of communities creating their own "Rule of Life," not unlike the rules monastic communities have used for centuries to shape their common life. With resources easily accessible and framed in a way that encourage creativity and contextualization, we prayed that the imaginations of Episcopalians would be sparked so that people everywhere would develop ways of inviting others into practices such as praying daily, reading scripture regularly, and engaging their faith in outward ways. None of us knew what the response would be from churches or individuals.

Leaders like Mary Bea—moved by the power of the Spirit—are now making that dream real. Shortly after hearing the presiding bishop's opening sermon at General Convention in July 2018, Mary Bea began investigating the Way of Love materials available online. After viewing Bishop Curry's five-minute video on the seven practices,[1] she knew she had found the foundation for her fall programs. Soon she had established a variety of small groups where forty participants could investigate the practices. Believing that daily reflections would ground her circles in claiming Jesus' way of love and assist them in recognizing how the practices were already woven into their daily lives, Mary Bea began to write. *Living the Way of Love . . .* is the result.

As chair of the Commission on Spirituality for the Diocese of Alabama, Mary Bea understood. "What the Presiding Bishop has done is brilliant: he has taken a sixteen-hundred-year-old concept and framed it for the

---

1. https://www.episcopalchurch.org/explore-way-love

twenty-first century. In the Way of Love practices, we have the wisdom of the Anglican monastic tradition in a framework that's doable for a mom in Mountain Brook, Alabama."[2]

Mary Bea anticipates that the forty people who participated in her groups this past year "are going to be engaged in the life of their faith community in ways we never would have imagined." Multiply this impact in Alabama by the number of groups gathering to engage the practices across the church and you begin to sense the potential leaven in the loaf and how people who are practicing become a power station for the Episcopal Church and beyond. Mary Bea describes it this way: "It feels like the Spirit is dancing in all these different places. Who could have imagined? It's melding a sense of movement— people saying 'yes' who don't even know each other. All those yeses are part of the way of love."

We say "Amen" and "Yes." Yes to the movement of local leaders who have taken the presiding bishop's invitation and run with it. Yes to the Spirit who is doing something bigger than all of us. Yes to everyone who has trusted and watched with gratitude. Yes to the generations of Anglicans before us who have lived the catholic tradition in the vernacular—taking our ancient, historic faith and reimagining it so it's alive in our contexts today. Yes to a movement of thousands of Episcopalians who are grow-

---

2. Mary Bea Sullivan, phone conversation with Courtney Cowart, December 3, 2018.

ing in faith and becoming leaven in the loaf, bearing new and intensified life across our church. We say "yes," trusting the Spirit has already said "yes" back.

Courtney V. Cowart, Executive Director of
The Society for the Increase of the Ministry

Stephanie Spellers, Canon to the Presiding Bishop
for Evangelism, Reconciliation, and Creation

Introduction

What do you most desire in your life today? A renewed prayer life? A deeper connection to Jesus? Balance? Clarity? Peace? I invite you to join me in this forty-day pilgrimage of practices for living the way of love. These practices can help us focus our energy on living the way Jesus lived—the way of powerful, liberating, redemptive, world-changing, unconditional love. A pilgrimage is a spiritual journey toward a desired destination. A pilgrimage requires taking time separate from everyday demands. My prayer is that your holy "yes" toward devoting some time each day to living a Jesus-centered life will take you closer to your desired destination.

The seed for this book came from watching an inspiring video of the Episcopal Church's 27th presiding bishop, Michael Curry, inviting us to claim, or reclaim, the Jesus-inspired practices "that can train up the spirit to follow in the way of Jesus and to look something like Jesus."[3] These biblically inspired practices are:

---

3. Presiding Bishop Michael Curry, "The Way of Love: Practices for a Jesus-Centered Life," The Episcopal Church, accessed December 3, 2018, www.episcopalchurch.org/explore-way-love.

Turn
Learn
Pray
Worship
Bless
Go
Rest

What follows are thirty-six brief daily reflections along with journaling prompts and spiritual exercises intended to support living a Jesus-centered life. Each of these reflections corresponds to one of the seven practices mentioned above. Days thirty-seven through forty offer reflections designed to help you identify the practices that are most important to you. Finally, the epilogue on page 111 provides guidance for creating your own "rule of life"—a framework of practices that are most effective in helping you find the Way of Love and walk its path. If you choose to use this book with companions in a small group, a facilitator guide can be downloaded at www.churchpublishing.org/livingthewayoflove.

A rule of life is a premise grounded in the Benedictine tradition. One author describes it this way, "The root meaning of the Latin and Greek words translated as 'rule' is *trellis*. Saint Benedict was not promulgating rules for living; he was establishing a framework on which a life can grow. While a branch of a plant climbing a trellis cannot go in any direction it wants, you cannot know in advance just which way it will go. The plant is finding its own path, within a structure. The space in which it moves is open, though not without boundaries."[4]

Esther de Waal writes, "St. Benedict never loses sight of the primacy of love; the Rule might almost be called a handbook on the practice of loving. That living out of love in its most practical terms, which we struggle with every day, hinges on our love of Christ, the keystone of it all."[5]

In preparation for beginning this pilgrimage, I encourage you to find a quiet spot to return to each day. Perhaps you will claim it as sacred and place a candle there. Carve out fifteen minutes to an hour each day to attune your heart to the heartbeat of God. You may wish to purchase a special journal for recording your thoughts. There are also spaces within these pages to jot down your immediate reflections following a few prompts.

In concluding his call to following in the way of love, Bishop Curry said, "The old hymn says it best, 'Breathe on me, breath of God, fill me with life anew, that I may love what thou dost love, and do what thou dost do.'"[6] Trust that taking this time to replenish your soul will strengthen your connection to God and positively impact the world in ways you may never know. Trust that God will respond

---

4. Patrick Henry, ed., *Benedict's Dharma: Buddhists Reflect on the Rule of Saint Benedict* (New York: Riverhead Books, 2001), 1.

5. Esther de Waal, *Seeking God: The Way of St. Benedict* (Collegeville, MN: Liturgical Press, 2001), 145.

6. Curry, "The Way of Love."

to your "holy yes" by growing you in the virtues of peace, patience, kindness, gentleness, and self-control; that you will grow in love of God and of neighbor.

God's peace,
Mary Bea Sullivan
November 2018

Author's note: Many stories are shared on these pages. I am grateful to those who entrusted their stories to me and to you and agreed for them to be included. When a child is mentioned, names have been changed. It is in the sharing of our stories that we grow in understanding of one another. We are all a part of the great story—God's and ours.

Standing in the Hog Trough

*I will get up and go to my father, and I will say to him,
"Father, I have sinned against heaven and before you."*
(Luke 15:18)

My friend and I were savoring fresh salads under the
patio umbrellas at one of our favorite eateries. It was a
rare, cool summer day in Birmingham. We were lament-
ing mistakes we had made and the challenge of coming
back from the big ones. Leaning forward, she declared,
"You know, it's only when you realize you are standing
in the hog trough that you can run back home to ask
forgiveness." Of course, she was alluding to the parable
of the prodigal son and the epiphany he experiences
after insulting his father, squandering his inheritance,
and sinking to the lowliest of jobs—feeding the pigs.
Ashamed, the son returns home to ask forgiveness (Luke
15:11–32).

What does standing in the hog trough mean to you? Is
it looking at your bank balance and realizing your spending signifies an unhealthy need for more stuff? Is it when
you find yourself staring across the table at a stranger,
even though you had vowed to honor and cherish that

person forever? Perhaps it is waking up with another hangover or with that gnawing feeling you get when you have said something unkind, yet again.

We've all had them, those seminal moments when we can no longer hide from the ways we have hurt God, ourselves, or others. Like the trough, those moments stink; they are uncomfortable, but they are invitations to live anew. Yes, the hog trough is dark and dirty, but it pales in comparison to the exuberant love of the father who sprints toward his smelly son with outstretched arms, pulling him close and covering him in kisses. Jesus tells us the father was ready to forgive before the request was even made.

Such is the love and grace and forgiveness of God toward us. If all we had were the messes, we would be without hope. Thankfully, at the core of Jesus's message is reassurance that God desires a relationship with us—faults and all. Even in the worst mess of our own making, God is with us:

> *When you pass through the waters, I will be with you; and through the rivers, they shall not overwhelm you; when you walk through fire you shall not be burned, and the flame shall not consume you.* (Isa. 43:2)

We need not remain paralyzed in the slop because we are loved and forgiven. I invite you to turn away from the trough and turn toward the grace of God's love and forgiveness.

Reflect

Describe a time you realized you were standing in the "hog trough." What helped you turn back toward God's love?

Perhaps you feel you are standing in it now. For what would you like to be forgiven? In what way do you desire to begin anew?

Listening to Scripture

"Listen carefully, my child, to the teaching of the master and bend close the ear of your heart." —Catherine Wybourne, OSB, Prologue of the Rule of Saint Benedict[7]

We were gathered in a circle for a woman's retreat, our attention drawn to the blue vase filled with wildflowers perched on the "altar" in the center. Gold-tinged votives flickering the light of the Christ adorned the "altar," which was draped in crocheted blankets created by the hands of women who have long since left this earth.

I began the instructions for the sacred practice of slowly digesting scripture called *lectio divina*—an ancient practice of praying the scriptures. During *lectio divina*, the practitioner listens to the text of the Bible with the "ear of the heart," as if he or she is in conversation with God, and God is suggesting the topics for

---

7. The opening sentence of the Prologue of the Rule of Saint Benedict. Catherine Wybourne, OSB translation. (Collegeville, MN: Liturgical Press, 2008), 221.

4

discussion.[8] *Lectio divina* may be practiced alone or in a small group.

After we completed the prayerful reading of scripture, one of the women responded, "The reading came alive for me. I usually read so fast, but going slowly and taking time for silence, it felt like it seeped into my heart in a deep way." Another person noticed, "I love that we read so much scripture on Sunday. Taking this small amount and lingering with it helped me to absorb it differently."

Reflect

Yesterday, we read about the opportunity to return to God when we find ourselves "standing in the hog trough." Today, you are invited to experience the "divine reading" (*lectio divina*) of a portion of that passage from Luke.

Slowly read aloud the following passage, taking time in silence after each reading:

- The first time, **listen with the ear of the heart** for a word or a phrase.

- The second time, **reflect** on how the word touches you in your life today.

---

8. Lectio Divina instructions from Contemplative Outreach Brochure, www.contemplativeoutreach.org/sites/default/files/documents/lectio _divina.pdf.

- The third time, **respond** spontaneously to any prayer or expression of the experience.

- The fourth time, **rest** in the word allowing space for God to speak to you in the silence.

But when he came to himself he said, "How many of my father's hired hands have bread enough and to spare, but here I am dying of hunger! I will get up and go to my father, and I will say to him, 'Father, I have sinned against heaven and before you; I am no longer worthy to be called your son; treat me like one of your hired hands.'" So he set off and went to his father. But while he was still far off, his father saw him and was filled with compassion; he ran and put his arms around him and kissed him. Then the son said to him, "Father, I have sinned against heaven and before you; I am no longer worthy to be called your son." But the father said to his slaves, "Quickly, bring out a robe—the best one—and put it on him; put a ring on his finger and sandals on his feet. And get the fatted calf and kill it, and let us eat and celebrate; for this son of mine was dead and is alive again; he was lost and is found!" And they began to celebrate. (Luke 15:17–24)

Perhaps you want to journal about what came to you in this time of sacred reading.

Giving Thanks

"For all things come of you, and of your own have we given you." (1 Chron. 29:14)

Huddled in the choir room—a pack of exuberant young children and me—our mission was to create Prayers of the People for an upcoming children's service. "Okay," I began, "one of the ways we pray is to give thanks to God for the many gifts God gives us." Sweet earnest eyes gazed back at me like sunflowers reaching toward the sun. Looks like those compel me to try and be a little better human being.

"I'm going to keep track of what you have to say and make a list. What are you thankful for?" Unprepared for the onslaught of appreciation which ensued, I scribbled as fast as I could. "My mom." "Scout, my dog." "Ice cream." "Chocolate ice cream." "Moose Tracks ice cream." "Alright, I've got ice cream down—we can assume all flavors are included. What else are you grateful for?"

Shouting over one another, their prayers of thanks rising through the rafters. "The sun." "My teachers." "I'm thankful that I hit the ball yesterday." "I'm thankful for the way the rain feels on my face." Wow! That one surprised me. The longer we steeped ourselves in gratitude, the more profound our perspective on that for which we were grateful became.

Gratitude does not mean that everything in our life is perfect; it is choosing to be content with our blessings instead of obsessing about what is missing. Gratitude unlocks the possibility for happiness and connects us with the Creator. Meister Eckhart said, "If the only prayer you say in your life is 'thank you,' it will be enough."[9]

Recently, I was with a woman who is in her nineties. She rarely leaves her home, others tend to her most basic needs. A fashion icon in her day, she has given away her jewels and cares not for new clothes. She has known loss—the loss of loved ones and the obvious loss of life-style and physical abilities. When I asked her how she was doing, she beamed, "Oh, I am so grateful." When I asked her to say more, she said, "I was explaining to a friend just the other day that even though I have had terribly sad things happen in my life, God always brought me to joy on the other side. It was horrible when my son died, and yet, I'm so glad I had him for as long as I did."

"To be grateful is to recognize the love of God in everything. . . . Every breath we draw is a gift. . . . Every moment of existence is a grace." —Thomas Merton , *Thoughts in Solitude,* 33 (1956)

---

9. Meister Eckhart (1260–1328) was a German theologian and Christian mystic.

Reflect

"What are you thankful for?"

I invite you to keep a gratitude journal for one week. List at least ten things for which you are thankful each day. Avoid duplicating previous entries.

Worship

Pray

Learn

Turn

DAY 4

Bless

Go

Rest

Kneeling at the Rail

We adore you, O Christ, and we bless you, because by your holy cross you have redeemed the world. (Book of Common Prayer, 281)

It was Good Friday and we were walking the Stations of the Cross in a field on the church's property. Solemnly, silently, we walked between each of the stations. The ground beneath our feet was uneven, requiring attention to assure not to turn an ankle or land in the dirt. At the conclusion of the final station, we continued into the church. Clergy knelt at the altar rail and the cross was draped across the rail, near me.

After the solemn collects were read, hushed silence cloaked the room. One at a time, people came forward to kiss or touch the cross, many with tear-stained faces. Finally, Gladys, one of the matriarchs of the congregation, came forward. Soft of body and fierce in faith, hers is an abiding in God steeped in joy and love and fresh grief. In the past nine months, she had buried two daughters and a husband. Where some of us would run from God in anger, Gladys runs toward God in trust.

As if transported to the evangelical church of her native Jamaica, Gladys raised her palms to the sky and began to pray to God aloud. Gratitude and love and trust poured out of that God-soaked soul. Gladys prayed for her biological family, for her church family, and then she prayed for me—her priest. She named my husband, my children, she asked God to give me all those qualities one would desire in a priest—courage, faith, wisdom, and love. Kneeling next to Gladys, who was kneeling next to the cross, I was aware that in that moment, she was our priest.

The liturgical rhythm of the seasons resonate because they illuminate the entire scope of human experience. Regular participation in worship provides a Christ-centered framework for living in all stages and seasons of our lives.

Reflect

What is most meaningful to you in worship?

What do you find challenging?

When was a time you were surprised by God in worship?

DAY 5

Pray · Worship · Bless · Learn · Go · Turn · Rest

Stories of Hope

"And you will have confidence, because there is hope; you will be protected and take your rest in safety." (Job 11:18)

The text read, "Want to go to coffee?" Normally, this would be just another nice invitation for time together with a friend. However, this friend had rarely ventured out for social engagements during the past year. Her husband had been diagnosed with cancer. They had entered into a self-imposed quarantine to avoid germs hoping that he wouldn't get sick and could stay on track with his treatments.

"Want to get coffee?" meant something more; it meant, "We're coming to the other side of this thing." It meant new life.

After a lengthy exchange about family and treatments and anything that gushed forth in our desire to reconnect, I asked my friend, "What did you learn that only this hard experience could have taught you?" Usually one to reflect before responding, my friend immediately said, "We love each other so much. We are closer than we have ever been before. I learned to take care of things he usually takes care of and he learned to let go and watch me do them in ways that were different than his." Pensive for a moment, she continued, "The hardest part is seeing him in pain. I can't fix that. I can only love him."

Days later I was on the phone with my mother, a devout Catholic who begins every day praying the rosary and often going to church for mass. Mom was recovering from a skin cancer treatment that was taking excruciatingly long to heal. The pain was severe, and my independent, strong-willed mother was being sidelined by mobility issues.

Toward the end of the conversation I said, "You know, Mom, if you were a parishioner, I might ask you, 'Where is God in this?'" Similar to my friend who had been caring for her husband, my mother responded without hesitation, "God is everywhere in this. When I feel the pain, I give thanks to God for the great life I have had. I think about how I'm eighty-six years old and how healthy I have been for most of my life. It makes me grateful. When I feel the pain, I offer it up to God."

Reflecting on these two encounters, I know that both my friend and my mother inspire me to seek the gifts that can come from difficult situations. Recognizing these gifts is not a surface-level response that denies the struggle. Cultivating eyes that can see gift in hard times comes from courageously acknowledging the struggle. These are eyes that have been steeped in prayer and gratitude before the hard times come.

Reflect

What challenges are you facing today?

Where are you afraid, or in pain? How might God be blessing you even in the midst of the struggle?

How might others be blessed if you humbly share your story?

Warming

*Then they also will answer, "Lord, when was it that we
saw you hungry or thirsty or a stranger or naked or sick
or in prison, and did not take care of you?" Then he will
answer them, "Truly I tell you, just as you did not do it
to one of the least of these, you did not do it to me."*
(Matt. 25:44–45)

Temperatures had dipped well below freezing for days
on end. Warming stations were set up throughout the
city to provide shelter for those living on the streets. The
community of Grace Episcopal Church in Woodlawn did
what they had always done—opened their doors.

Grace Church is in the epicenter of the poverty earthquake. However, rather than withdraw into a mentality of
scarcity, this congregation, which is often stretched thin,
gives sacrificially. Every day they feed those who are hungry. Every day they clothe those who are naked. Every day
they pray with those wrestling with the ravages of mental
illness.

After weeks of providing shelter, a plea was issued via
social media, "Grace Woodlawn needs volunteers to staff
their warming station." The small, generous congregation

couldn't do it all on their own. Congregants had to go to work, take care of their children, tend to their lives. They couldn't possibly spend another night on a cot or hand out another cup of cocoa. We, in the greater community, were summoned to provide relief.

Our home is nearly equidistant to Grace Woodlawn and the parish where I serve, Saint Luke's in Mountain Brook, Alabama. We are 2.8 miles to Grace and 2.6 miles to Saint Luke's. The experiences of those living in these two communities are worlds apart. Although our home is in the middle, our lives trend more toward the Saint Luke's world than that of Grace Woodlawn.

My husband, Malcolm, and I signed up for a mere two-hour slot on a Friday afternoon. Malcolm is a frequent celebrant for "Church in the Park," a weekly service dedicated to providing Good News and good food to those living in the margins. Malcolm is at home with the homeless. He comfortably chatted with the men—meeting them as equals, honoring their inherent dignity.

More than one of the men and women said to me, "Thank you, ma'am, for your help." Or, "We are so grateful to this church and the community. You are a lifesaver." I was humbled knowing that what I was giving was insignificant in comparison to their gratitude, and to the sacrifices made by others.

Most of my time was spent talking to Mother Robyn, the rector at Grace Woodlawn. She told me how Kay, their "deacon-in-training," had spent every night on a cot and every day at work. I learned how Robyn's community had been cooking and serving and loving those who needed shelter. When I pointed out to Robyn, with a voice not free of guilt, how different our lives are—me a priest at a well-resourced congregation, and she the priest at Grace Woodlawn, she immediately responded. "There isn't anywhere else I want to be. My life here isn't perfect, and I get frustrated, but I love my people, and I will always be on the side of the least of these." No heroics, no smug sense of self-importance, no judgment of my privileged life. "There isn't anywhere else I *want* to be."

Malcolm and I walked toward our car at the end of our shift and bumped into Jim and Nancy, Saint Luke's parishioners who had come to provide comfort and support—smiling, generous human bridges in the divide between two worlds. I knew from previous conversations that they had started a nonprofit in another state, an organization that provides backpacks filled with food for thousands of hungry students. Later they shared with me how much their evening at Grace Church meant to them—how they were inspired by the joyful, multigenerational Muslim community that provided dinner that evening.

As is always the case, my encounters at Grace Church Woodlawn and whenever I *think* I am showing up to support someone else, it is I who benefits greatly. There is no romanticizing the horrors of poverty and of violence. Yet, my chance meetings with those who walk bravely into the darkness, shining the light of Christ, continue to inspire me to be mindful of those whose lives are different from mine, to listen and learn from them.

Reflect

Where are you being encouraged to "show up"?

Is there a community or a person that is living in circumstances different from your own that you would like to connect with? Learn from? Perhaps you are drawn to collaborate on a project that will benefit those in need.

Freedom

"Six days shall work be done; but the seventh day is a sabbath of complete rest, a holy convocation; you shall do no work: it is a sabbath to the Lord throughout your settlements." (Lev. 23:3)

Assuming we would forget, God gave us a day to remember that we are free and that we are God's beloved people. Sabbath was a gift from God to a people who had been oppressed. It was a reminder to the Israelites that they were free—free to rest and free to worship. Neither of which were available to them in captivity.

Years ago when I started an end-of-life care nonprofit, Project Compassion, I found it impossible to rest. Mind racing with creative ideas, or funding woes, or the burden of unanswered e-mails, I would frequently rise at 4:00 a.m. and begin my day. When I wasn't working, I was tending to the life of our family. It seemed everyone had a piece of me except for God, and for me.

My zest to change the world became "the bread of anxious toil" and it showed in the way that I treated people. My children became the recipients of sharp admonitions. My husband was given little grace when he made mistakes.

One day a dear friend called to ask if we could go for a walk to talk about something that was weighing on her. We were usually accompanied by our dogs on our treks, but she indicated there were to be no distractions for this conversation. Our feet barely hit the trail before she blurted out, "You are being so unkind to James, I am afraid it is undermining all of the good we are trying to do." Ouch! "Besides, he doesn't deserve to be spoken to that way. No one does."

I was indignant. How could anyone question my motives or the way I was treating others in the organization? I had *started* this thing. It couldn't manage without me. And yet, this was a friend who had given as much or more to the organization than I had. This was a friend who was a *cheerleader,* an *encourager.* Rarely, if ever, had I heard her express herself in this way.

After the initial sting of the rebuke faded, trusting the source, I took time to reflect. I realized my busyness had made me toxic. Resentment and ego and grief and self-importance and worry and ambition had created a noxious stew within me. Unchecked by those things which usually ground me, like time in prayer, or undistracted space with the people I love, or doing things that bring me joy, I had forgotten who I was. I had forgotten Whose I was. This hard wake-up call was a gift, a reminder that I am free at least one day a week from the stresses of work, and that I am God's beloved—even when I'm acting like a jerk.

"To allow oneself to be carried away by a multitude of conflicting concerns, to surrender to too many demands, to commit oneself to too many projects, to want to help everyone in everything is to succumb to violence. The frenzy of the activist neutralizes his or her work for peace." —Thomas Merton[10]

Reflect

Are you stressed out? Or are you experiencing a sense of contentment with your work/life balance? If you are stretched, who is impacted by your overwork? How?

What one thing might you say "no" to that will allow a "yes" to time in prayer, rest, and/or an activity that brings you joy?

What one thing would you love to do if you designated time for sabbath rest? Give yourself the gift of an hour, or half a day, or a whole day tending to sabbath.

---

10. Thomas Merton, *Conjectures of a Guilty Bystander* (New York: Penguin Random House, 1968), 81.

Beauty in the Rubble

My thoughts are not your thoughts, nor are your ways my ways, says the Lord. (Isa. 55:8)

When I was attending Virginia Theological Seminary, a number of my classmates went to help in the Northeast after Hurricane Sandy. They were moved by many stories. The most memorable one for me was about two brothers living in New York City. They had been estranged for decades. Enmity made it impossible for them to be in the same room together.

After the storm subsided, the older brother trudged down the hill to his brother's flooded neighborhood. Heartbreaking devastation increased with each block the man descended. Eventually, he found his younger brother waiting for help in his uninhabitable home. "Will you come and live with me until your home is repaired?" the older brother asked. Together, they walked to higher ground.

When we are knocked off-center, compassion can flow from that humble place. We are reminded that we are not in control. But God, God is so powerful that God can make good from anything, using the most surprising mechanisms in ways we cannot imagine. A gorge's beauty comes from centuries of a powerful river carving away a mountain. Forgiveness flows, old resentments subside from hearts broken open by tragedy. The challenge is living in that place of generosity and remembering our vulnerable solidarity with one another every day.

Reflect

Part of our regular returning to God is letting go of old resentments. What are you holding on to that eats away at you? How does that sap energy from your life?

If you knew you only had days, weeks, or months to live, what relationship(s) would you attempt to mend? What one step could you make in that direction today?

Wrestling Together

Your word is a lamp to my feet and a light to my path.
(Ps. 119:105)

Years ago I was in a Bible study with the Rev. Rick Edens when I asked him how we really know how to interpret the Bible. A portion of his thoughtful answer went something like this: "We wrestle with the Word in community because it is in coming together we come closer to the truth. By challenging one another, we check ourselves from making the Bible and God in our own image. The intention that we bring to that time together is important too. Are we truly seeking a deeper understanding of God in our studying together?"

Those words were one of the crumbs on the trail that brought me back to organized religion. I knew I needed others to seek a truth bigger than me. There are gifts and challenges in gathering regularly with others to wrestle with scripture, or a piece of literature, or to share the joys and challenges of our lives.

We can find comfort sharing our stories and realizing we are not alone. Wisdom is gleaned from listening to others' experiences. Laughter is louder and deeper when

24

shared. I have been in groups where I, or someone in the group, is challenged by another participant. Perspectives might be dramatically different, one person may dominate the conversation, or may be insensitive to the needs of others.

It has been my own experience that frequently these difficult participants have the most to teach me. If I pay close attention and bring my irritation to prayer, oftentimes these individuals are mirroring unattractive aspects of myself. Or perhaps they are behaving in a way that is similar to that of someone in my life with whom I have unfinished business.

Reflect

What is your experience in learning more about God with others? Do you seek out groups or at least one or two others to wrestle with the Word in relation to life's challenges?

If you were to consider some of those difficult souls in your life as messengers from God, what might they be teaching you? What scripture passage might be helpful in understanding where God is in the struggle?

Morning Prayer

Evening and morning and at noon I utter my complaint and moan, and he will hear my voice. (Ps. 55:17)

We know from Psalm 55:17 and from Daniel 6:10 that there was an ancient tradition of praying to God at fixed times throughout the day. Imagine Jesus, a devout Jew, stopping at preordained times of the day to pray. Today, monastics pray together starting before the rise of the sun until after it has set. We may join those throughout the world praying in this way. The Daily Office in the Book of Common Prayer (BCP) provides a rhythm for us to pause and pray throughout the day—"Praying the Hours." Thomas Cranmer, an author and compiler of the first Book of Common Prayer published in 1549, was influenced by the Benedictine monastic tradition which emphasized Praying the Hours.

Beginning our days with Morning Prayer—confessing our transgressions, reading the lectionary (assigned scripture for the day), lifting our cares, concerns, and thanksgivings to God—sets our hearts in the direction we desire to go. Even though we may lose sight of that direction by midmorning, beginning our days in this way helps to cultivate good soil from which God can grow us.

How can we reclaim this ancient practice of pausing throughout the day? How will that impact our yearning for Jesus as the center of our lives?

Reflect

Pray Morning Prayer. It may seem daunting if you have not learned how, but simply follow the italicized instructions as you go, and do not worry about mistakes. What is most important is the intention of your prayer. If you prefer traditional language, use Rite I (BCP, 37); for more contemporary language, Rite II (BCP, 75). Ask an experienced friend or a clergyperson for help if you've not prayed from the BCP before.

There are many resources to assist praying the Daily Office—Morning Prayer, Noonday Prayer, Evening Prayer, and Compline.

- You may access the BCP online: www.bcponline.org.

- You may listen to the daily office at: www.missionstclare.com/english/index.html.

- You may purchase a Book of Common Prayer (1979) through any book seller.

- Find lectionary readings at: http://satucket.com/lectionary/.

- There are apps available as well, including the Book of Common Prayer, Mission St. Clare, and Electronic Common Prayer (eCP).
- If you are pressed for time, simply pray the morning Daily Devotions for Individuals and Families (BCP, 137).

The Front Row Seat No One Wants

Blessed be the God and Father of our Lord Jesus Christ, the Father of mercies and the God of all consolation, who consoles us in all our affliction, so that we may be able to console those who are in any affliction with the consolation with which we ourselves are consoled by God. (2 Cor. 1:3–4)

We seat them last and give them a place of honor before the funeral begins. Oftentimes, in the South especially, the congregation stands as they enter.

I like to think of standing for the family as a gesture of honor, but also more. It is an outward and visible sign of a promise to stand with them in the hours, days, months, and lifetimes ahead as they wrestle with their new normal—a life where their loved one is no longer physically present.

Our coming together is important—to remember people who have meant something to us, to grieve, and to celebrate the first and last and all of the breaths in between, of people who have meant something to us. For those in the front row seat that no one wants, it can be healing to share stories, to pray, to be comforted by the reverberations of the organ and the singing voices.

We place tissues in their pews, knowing they may cry. Some don't; perhaps their pillow was soaked the night before, and the ducts are dry. Others are too shocked to feel anything. Maybe the relationship was difficult and it is hard to know what to grieve—the love that never came, the unhealed wounds, or the loss of hope for reconciliation. Bitter tastes especially rank in that front row.

Perhaps the last few years or months have been filled with suffering. So maybe there is relief, joy even, knowing the "strife is over."

We place bulletins on their pews so they may follow the service if they like. Some follow every word, drawing comfort in the familiar prayers and song. Others, heads swimming and foggy from lost sleep, or with that nagging pain in the gut, seem to wish it would all be over so they can return to the safety of their covers. For those who worship in other ways, or not all, the ritual can be surprisingly soothing. Or it can be jarringly uncomfortable, only adding to overwhelming pain.

There is no correct way to occupy the front row seat that no one wants. Most of us will spend some time there, though. And not one of us will escape being the one remembered.

Funerals and memorial services are only a small part of how we worship. But it is a critical time in which we come together as a community to support and love one another. They also serve as important reminders to our finitude—an opportunity to reevaluate if we are living according to our values.

Reflect

How do you want to prepare your front-row folks for the day they will remember you?

What do you want to make sure you say to those most important to you?

Are there things you wish to do while you are still living?

How do you "stand with" people who are grieving? Is it difficult to go to funerals? Is it natural to show up with a listening ear or a warm meal?

Grief is a part of life. Without any self-judgment consider the role grief plays in your relationships, and how coming together in worship helps or hinders your ability to support others who are experiencing pain.

Smilin' Uphill

Rejoice in the Lord always; again I will say, Rejoice.
(Phil. 4:4)

I love running in our neighborhood. Large oak and maple trees adorn the sidewalks. Early twentieth-century homes provide interesting distractions from the aches and pains of my aging body. What I don't love are the abundance of hills. There is no avoiding them. The toughest one is on the return trip toward home on my running route.

This morning as I approached the long climb, I spotted a man walking on the sidewalk ahead of me. This is not uncommon, as this is a popular and scenic route. What was uncommon was his smile—broad and unabashedly friendly. From all outward appearances, he and I are very different—he a man, I a woman; he a person of color, I Caucasian; he in his seventies or so, I in my fifties.

But that smile, that beaming and generous and encouraging smile, made me smile too. It lit up my insides and warmed my weary legs. Nearly everyone I pass on my route I acknowledge in some way. Many nod, some eke out a "hi," but few return a smile; and rarely one so bright.

Powered by this stranger's warm greeting, I trekked up the hill with more energy to my step.

I decided to smile for the remainder of my run. Even when no one was nearby, I turned up the corner of my lips and smiled. It took a bit of energy to exercise those muscles along with my legs and lungs. Yet it gave me vitality to face the hills ahead.

Reflect

What would it be like if we were more intentional about blessing others with spontaneous smiles? How can we better face steep difficulties if we consider smiling our way through at least some of them?

Intentionally smile at least ten times today—share at least half of them with others and save a few for yourself. Keep track on your phone. How did it impact you and others when you smiled?

Scripture gives us insight into a cheerful countenance. Consider these: Psalm 96, Psalm 126:2, Proverbs 17:22.

Bags of Comfort

"Blessed are those who mourn, for they will be comforted."
(Matt. 5:4)

Clad in matching gold T-shirts with their church's logo on the back, twenty-five third graders earnestly strode into the pastoral care office at UAB Hospital. Flanked by their children's minister and parent chaperones, these children were on a mission—to provide comfort to families who had a loved one in the Intensive Care Unit (ICU).

They had been well prepared for what awaited them; they had learned about compassion and the power of prayer in difficult times; they assembled comfort bags containing gum, candy, tissues, minijournals, and pens.

Teams of children were assigned to different ICUs. A hospital chaplain and an adult member of their congregation accompanied each of the teams. Some sheepishly, others boldly, approached weary, worried souls in the waiting rooms. Handing out bags of comfort, they would say things like, "We want you to know we are praying for you and your loved one." Or, "This is so you will know that God is with you." Surprised smiles greeted the children.

In one of the waiting rooms, a small boy approached a large family. As he passed out his bags, he asked about their family member. "Would you like us to pray?" this four-foot-something ambassador-for-Christ inquired. "Yes!" was the resounding reply. They circled up; the child led them in prayer. Fervently, he prayed for comfort and strength and healing. Tears streaked each cheek— tears of sadness, tears of gratitude, tears of hope—for it was a little child who led them.

"Encouraging children to be kind has much more impact than just being helpful; research shows that kindness can have positive effects on health, self-esteem, and even happiness."[11] Dr. Michele Borba suggests ways to help teach your child kindness is to show kindness, expect and value it, and explain it.

Reflect

How can you help children in your life to be more kind?

Where can you go and intentionally provide kindness? What boundaries might need to be crossed?

---

11. Kylie Rymanowicz, "Children and Empathy: Kindness," Michigan State University, May 4, 2017, http://msue.anr.msu.edu/news/children_and_empathy_kindness.

Body Wisdom

Thus says the Lord: Stand at the crossroads, and look, and ask for the ancient paths, where the good way lies; and walk in it, and find rest for your souls. (Jer. 6:16)

Noticing the frenetic pace at which I was bustling through the halls, the thought crossed my mind, *I need to slow down.* Later that same evening, while entering the house—jostling groceries, a laptop, and mail, a similar insight zoomed across the screen, *I am carrying too much.*

The next morning I arrived at the gym a few minutes late for an interval training class. A young woman approached me and reprimanded my tardiness. "Usually we lock the door when the class begins." She said in her most *hey I'm in charge* voice, "When people are late, they miss the demonstrations and the stretching—they can get hurt." Puffing up in my most dismissive, *hey I've got a few decades on you* voice, I responded, "Thanks, don't worry about me—I've done this class many times and will be fine."

Assigned to station #1—dead leg lifts, I bent my legs, leaned over from a standing position, and lifted two eighteen-pound dumbbells. On the third repetition, a zing shot straight up my back. I had been here before.

I knew what this meant. Trying to avoid contorting my face too much, I approached the bossy middle school–looking instructor and told her I had to leave. Humiliated, I gingerly exited only minutes after entering the gym. Fortunately (or unfortunately), because I had experienced this more than once before, I knew what my back needed—rest.

Jesus was *embodied, incarnate.* Bodies must be important. Our bodies carry a wisdom we ignore at our peril. All creatures require rest. I have a colleague who is public about the daily nap he takes on the couch in his office. He claims it is vital for him to maintain clarity throughout the day. How I need to follow his example and listen to my body.

Reflect

Even God rested. Perhaps, like my colleague, you are intentional about daily rest. Or maybe you have a weekly routine of sabbath-taking. How do you incorporate rest into your life?

If you have none, what might be a way you could claim rest in your life? How would you and those around you benefit from surrendering to your divinely inspired need for rest?

The Beauty in the Bark

They said to each other, "Were not our hearts burning within us while he was talking to us on the road, while he was opening the scriptures to us?" (Luke 24:32)

"I've brought some books to help us decide which trees and plants we want to plant in the yard," said Jim, an experienced arborist we hired to relandscape our yard. Things had gotten out of control after years of inattention. We loved the home, a recent purchase, but not this lack of "curb appeal."

Jim and I were sitting at our long farmhouse table. The kitchen was bright and open with ample windows providing a view of the densely wooded lot that surrounded us. When we hired Jim, I just wanted to give him a budget and let him "do his thing." But he insisted I participate by understanding my options and expressing my preferences.

Jim had arrived with an armload of horticulture books and laid them out on the table. Excitedly, he grabbed a large hardbound volume with pictures of each specimen in all seasons. "I would like for us to plant this paperbark maple outside of your living room window," Jim bubbled out. Lost in wonder, he pored over the pages of pictures of paperbark maple. "Look! This is what the bark looks like. Isn't it exquisite?"

Honestly, I had never considered the qualities of tree bark to this degree. An avid hiker and outdoorswoman, I am sure I had appreciated bark in an inconsequential kind of way, but Jim was *passionate* about bark. "What I love about this tree is that in the winter, in the time when we often think our yards are boring or dead-looking, paperbark maple *comes alive*. Leaves out of the way, we can see the deepest beauty this tree has to offer."

Of course, now I wanted that paperbark maple in front of my living room window. Jim was right; the bark that curled off of its trunk was fascinating. I envisioned myself savoring a cup of warm tea in the wintertime, waiting for the kids to come down the street, my eyes resting upon this wonder of nature.

Jim and I spent the next few hours studying pictures of many tree and plant species, taking care to consider how they would look in all four seasons. He drew a sketch of what would be blooming when, taking care to note the beauty of each specimen beyond the bloom.

If we were to believe that God has planted a seed of passion in us, perhaps we would give ourselves permission to pursue it. One of the many lessons that Jim taught me is that when I turn toward the pull of that which I love, my excitement and love of it is contagious. Perhaps you are yearning for more meaning and purpose in your life. Maybe too often we believe that it should manifest itself in grandiose ways—and that is true sometimes.

However, more often than not, the yearning is met not in setting the world on fire, but setting our hearts on fire.

That morning soaked in sweet revelry of tree bark and hellebores' blooms was eighteen years and six homes ago. Just this morning, as I traipsed up the long hill near our current home, I noticed the bark on a neighbor's crepe myrtle and thought of Jim. I sent blessing and gratitude his way and hoped he was still alive. Last I saw of him, some fifteen years ago, he was in treatment for cancer so I do not know if he is still with us. But, as long as I am breathing, his ability to see beauty in winter bark will live on.

Reflect

When have you noticed yourself most excited and energized? Where do you find joy and passion?

Give yourself the luxury of time to turn your attention toward what brings you the most joy, and explore it through prayer, conversation with a friend, or journaling. If you already are immersed in this passion, give thanks to God for the ability and the willingness to do so. If you rarely or infrequently explore this passion, what might you do to make space to grow the seed that God has planted in you?

The Word Comes Alive

The grass withers, the flower fades; but the word of our God will stand forever. (Isa. 40:8)

"The culmination of our work together will be for each of us to memorize and embody significant portions of scripture for a presentation to the entire seminary community." Panic set in as I heard Dr. Ruthanna Hooke proclaim the requirements for what would paradoxically become one of my favorite classes in seminary.

I've never been great at memorization. And yet, the idea of "biblical storytelling" was compelling. Every day I devoted a disproportionate amount of time on the homework for this *elective* class. Eventually, I was able to memorize more and more.

Awakened by immersion in the creation story, I noticed my surroundings in fresh ways. Walking through the lush grove of the seminary, I savored nascent oak leaves unfurling and squirrels scurrying. God's word written on my heart, the miracle of the generative nature of the Creator surprised me anew. Weeks into the class, I was practicing the Genesis passage yet again when I came to, "Then God said, 'Let us make humankind in our image, according to our likeness.'" Unanticipated tears streamed down my cheeks. *God so loves US, God made us to be in relationship with God.*

The evening of our presentation came. We, a small band of students ranging in age from twenty-five to sixty, clad in black, told portions of God's story from creation to Revelation. All of the practice, teamwork, and study poured out as offering. Grief contorted the faces of some in the audience when the entire ensemble embodied the Israelites in captivity as depicted in Psalm 137. Laughter erupted when Melinda comically portrayed Ananias's response to being called by God to go to Saul, the persecutor of the Jews, and *lay his hands on him.* At the conclusion, the gathered community rose to their feet with applause. I remember that moment, not as a personal, or even a communal triumph; I remember it as a time when scripture jumped off of the page and God's voice came alive.

Reflect

Is there a passage of scripture that you have memorized that is important to you? What is it and why? If not, choose a short piece of scripture to memorize. Tape this passage to your mirror, make a note on your phone. Find some time each day to be with it, study it, memorize it, embody it. If none come to mind, below are a few suggestions.

Beloved, let us love one another, because love is from God; everyone who loves is born of God and knows God. (1 John 4:7)

Create in me a clean heart, O God, and put a new and right spirit within me. (Ps. 51:10)

Perhaps you want to get your Bible and look up the following passages; maybe one of them is the one you want to memorize and desire God to write upon your heart.

Mark 12:28–31
Psalm 23
John 4:13–14

Walking Our Prayers

Many peoples shall come and say, "Come, let us go up to the mountain of the Lord, to the house of the God of Jacob; that he may teach us his ways and that we may walk in his paths." (Isa. 2:3a)

Walking at a brisk pace, Malcolm and I came upon a stunning outdoor labyrinth. The slate path bordered by ornamental grasses created an urban sanctuary even while cars and joggers passed by. We slowed our pace and walked our prayers. Beside the labyrinth entrance is a bronze plaque inscribed:

> *Ask, and*
> *it will be*
> *given to you.*
> *Seek, and*
> *you will find.*
> *Knock, and*
> *the door will be*
> *opened to you.*

The labyrinth is an ancient, meditative practice of walking our prayers. One way to walk the labyrinth is to carry something small in your hand. The item may represent a prayer or intention that you bring to the sacred path. When reaching the center, you may leave the object there, praying a prayer of release—setting it down and trusting God has got it.

I selected a smooth rock and stood at the entrance praying for the grace to let go of busyness, to discern the holy "yes" and the holy "no." Mindfully placing one foot in front of the other, occasionally passing my beloved on the path, stress and struggle and striving melted out— sacred offerings to the ground. How many others had walked their prayers on this site? How many diagnoses and broken hearts and grateful hearts beat this path? When I reached the middle, I paused and prayed and left my stone, hands free to swing by my side for the return pilgrimage.

I know of a woman who brought her grandchildren to walk an indoor labyrinth on Ash Wednesday. Her nine-year-old grandson was especially intent, pausing in the center, and walking back out. When asked about his experience, he responded, "It was like a force field of love and harmony . . . a giant circle of peace. I was protected from all of the hate in the world."

Reflect

Is there a labyrinth that you could walk and pray? For more information go to https://labyrinthlocator.com or www.veriditas.org.

Finger labyrinths can be purchased online, or you may download one at https://labyrinthsociety.org/download-a-labyrinth.

If you'd like to walk your prayers and do not have a labyrinth easily accessible, perhaps you could find a small token to take with you and go for a walk with the intention of praying with your feet in the way described above. Set your token down as you turn back and head toward home.

Selves, Souls, Bodies

Do not worry about anything, but in everything by prayer and supplication with thanksgiving let your requests be made known to God. (Phil. 4:6)

The term "Eucharist" comes from the Greek word *eucharistia,* which means "thanksgiving." When we gather for Holy Eucharist, we come for countless reasons—for solace, companionship, an encounter with the Holy, forgiveness, renewal, hope. Sometimes we come because it is what we have always done. We come ravenous to receive the Holy Food and Drink, sustenance for the life ahead.

Before we march or roll our way toward the rail, we pray our prayers of thanksgiving. "We give thanks to you, O God, for the goodness and love which you have made known to us in creation."[12] Yes! Thank you for the birds. Thank you for dirt and the vegetation that springs forth from it—for air, and sky, and sun. Oh we give thanks for life-giving rain.

---

12. Rite II, Book of Common Prayer, 368.

Continuing we pray, "in the calling of Israel to be your people; in your Word spoken through the prophets; and above all in the Word made flesh, Jesus, your Son." There is no response worthy of this gift—the sacrificial, life-giving love of Jesus. And yet we respond with a "thank you" that rumbles, rooted in the belly. We are reminded to respond with all that we are when we say, "And we earnestly desire thy fatherly goodness to accept this our sacrifice of praise and thanksgiving; . . . [W]e offer and present unto thee, O Lord, our selves, our souls and bodies."[13]

Here it is, God—me, my imperfect life—I give it all, in thanksgiving for it all. Thanks for the grace, love, forgiveness, challenges, and the disappointments that have called forth qualities before unknown. I give thanks for the reminder of dependence upon you alone.[14] I give you thanks.

Reflect

If you regularly attend Eucharist, pay particular attention to the prayers this week. Perhaps you want to close your books and eyes and let the beauty of the liturgy wash over you. What new words or thoughts touch you?

---

13. Rite I, Book of Common Prayer, 335, 336.

14. Inspired by "A General Thanksgiving" in the Book of Common Prayer, 836.

If you have been away from communal worship, will you risk a return? Sometimes that takes courage. Pray for courage, and the reception you receive will be warm.

Breathing Out Blessings

Then the Lord God formed man from the dust of the ground, and breathed into his nostrils the breath of life; and the man became a living being. (Gen. 2:7)

We were in our row of folding chairs at Saint Mary's Catholic Church. My sixth-grade mind tuning out a sermon that seemed to have little intersection with my life. An awareness beyond my experience, beyond me, enfolded me. Attuned to my breathing, I paid attention to each in-breath and each out-breath. Something I hadn't much considered before—breathing—became the object of absorption. It was as if I could see each breath in and each breath out.

Oddly, I realized that the breath I was breathing out was being breathed in by those around me. And then, the visceral experience that the air being breathed in and breathed out by the entire congregation was that which had been exhaled and inhaled by all of the others. Before the term "interdependence" became a thing I knew, it breathed its way into my young consciousness.

In his book *Sacred Fire: A Vision for a Deeper Human and Christian Maturity,* Ronald Rolheiser writes, "The air we breathe out into the universe is the air we will reinhale."[15]

Reflect

Take a few moments to observe the natural rhythm of your breathing. Close your eyes. Place your hands upon your belly—a place many of us judge; give that judgment a rest. Notice the air entering your nostrils, the rise of your belly, and the air traveling back up your trachea and out your nostrils. Stay with your breath for a few minutes.

Then consider:

What am I breathing out into the world?
How do I breathe out blessing? How do I breathe out curse?
What am I breathing back in?

When you feel complete, give thanks for every breath you have breathed and the many, or few, left to come.

Finally, pray for the awareness to bring blessing this day.

---

15. Ronald Rolheiser, *Sacred Fire: A Vision for a Deeper Human and Christian Maturity* (New York: Image, 2014), 241.

Christ's Light

"I will give you as a light to the nations, that my salvation may reach to the end of the earth." (Isa. 49:6b)

"On election day, 2016 . . . I found out that I have Frontotemporal Degeneration," explained Tracey Lind. Until her diagnosis, she had been the dean of Trinity Cathedral in Cleveland. A lover of words, Tracey confessed the struggle she now has to retrieve them. An avid hiker, she grieved the new shuffle in her walk. An extrovert, she is overwhelmed in crowds.

The audience trained our collective eye on Tracey. Rare is the opportunity to learn from someone who is experiencing dementia. Ever the teacher, she couldn't leave this lesson to someone else. With heroic effort, Tracey articulated living with dementia "from-the-inside-out." Joining her was Emily Ingalls, her wife who is a professional in her own right; Emily now refers to herself as "CLO" or "Chief Logistics Office." Emily's new vocation is to manage a life and home turned upside down by dementia.

Tracey spoke of cycling through a "washing machine" of emotions. Emily admitted being stuck in the anger cycle. Tracey has a desire "to make this dementia experience a pilgrimage." Emily laments the loss of her marriage as she had known it; some days of feeling more like "mommy" and less like "wife."

We marveled at their honesty and sacrificial love. Someone asked, "How would you manage without Emily?" Tears welled up, "I can't imagine it." She gazed upon her beloved who gazed back. In that moment, those two beating hearts, broken open by the undesired, unexpected diagnosis of dementia, opened our hearts—to our own loves, and our own losses.

Tracey and Emily are able to transform their pain by making meaning from it. For as long as they can, they will go into the world and vulnerably share their story. The canyon broken open in their hearts is shining the light of Christ on those with whom they encounter. Richard Rohr identifies the two primary paths of transformation into God as great love and great suffering. Both love and suffering crack our hearts wide open. At its best, the light of Christ shines through this brokenness.

Reflect

Where have you experienced great love, great loss?

How has that impacted your ability to go and be with others in pain?

Where might God be beckoning you to take that light of love and loss out into the world?

Airplane Mode

"Come to me, all of you that are weary and are carrying heavy burdens, and I will give you rest." (Matt. 11:28)

"Do you think you could turn that thing off for a little while?" my naturally patient husband asked, with more than a little irritation in his voice. After miles of conversation interrupted by texts buzzing and e-mail clearing, he was tired of sharing me with the undesired company of those on the other end of my iPhone. We were supposed to be getting away for some well-needed rest together. Yet, I was tethered to a device that does not promote rest or encourage encounters with those with whom we are present.

Realizing the world would continue to orbit without me responding to every inquiry, aware that I was wasting rare time alone with Malcolm, I put the phone on "airplane mode."

I have become enamored with "airplane mode." It is more effective than "silencing" our phones because there are no distracting indicators. Need to write? Airplane mode. Want to enjoy a fun game with family? Airplane mode. Pray? Airplane mode.

You get it. We are free from our technology when we create boundaries around it. If we make ourselves ever available, we train the world to creep in at will. Claiming technology-free space boosts our ability to be more focused, more effective, more present. More loving.

Reflect

In his book *Sabbath: Finding Rest, Renewal, and Delight in Our Busy Lives,* Wayne Muller uses the metaphor of a fence for creating boundaries around our time of sabbath. As you consider technology in your life, would you say that you manage it, or it manages you? What "fences" could you put around technology?

Technology can be a means to enhance our connection to God through online resources and apps. How does technology help you live a more Jesus-centered life? How does it get in the way of that life?

How can you incorporate rest from technology today? Every day? Every week?

Listen Devoutly

"Let anyone with ears to hear listen!" (Mark 4:23)

Adorned in a brightly colored scarf and burnt orange lipstick, Martha oozed artist. Her calm demeanor and kind smile evoked trust. This was good, since we who were gathered were fresh from our grief.

Martha suggested we share our experiences using the "Wisdom Circle" format. Adapted from a Native American tradition, this is a way for each person to speak from the heart without interruption. One of the instructions for the Wisdom Circle is to "listening devoutly." Martha explained the meaning of that strange and glorious term.

"Listening devoutly means listening with your whole being. There is no interrupting, no cross-talk. Also, when we listen devoutly we notice our judgments and let them be. That's tricky, listening without judgment. Receive the story from the other as gift without trying to judge or fix. Finally, avoid the natural desire to rehearse in your head what you wish to say when it is your turn to speak."

Following Martha's instructions, we shared our experiences of loss. Sacred silence enveloped the circle in between each precious story. Seldom had I paid attention in such a vigilant way. Rarely had I felt so heard. Christ's presence was palpable. We entered strangers; we parted companions.

I have employed the Wisdom Circle methodology countless times in facilitating small groups. This format promotes respectful listening and understanding diverse points of view. Once, a small group of us were making a contentious, critical decision for a parish. After nine months of discernment, incorporating the Wisdom Circle format at each gathering, the group, which had been divided, came to consensus. The parish flourished. Essential truths previously concealed by rigidity, busyness, or noise are revealed in shared silence and devout listening.

Our listening skills can be trained like muscles we exercise at the gym. One way to exercise our listening skills is to pay attention to the people right in front of us—they embody Jesus. We return to Jesus when we turn our full attention to another and listen with a willingness to be changed.

Reflect

When have you felt heard? How did that impact you?

When you are listening to others, do you regularly pay close attention not only to their words, but to the meaning and emotions beneath the words?

What distracts you from listening? What supports being present in this way?

Today, intentionally listen devoutly to another.

Meeting Jesus

They came to Jericho. As he and his disciples and a large crowd were leaving Jericho, Bartimaeus son of Timaeus, a blind beggar, was sitting by the roadside. When he heard that it was Jesus of Nazareth, he began to shout out and say, "Jesus, Son of David, have mercy on me!" Many sternly ordered him to be quiet, but he cried out even more loudly, "Son of David, have mercy on me!" Jesus stood still and said, "Call him here." And they called the blind man, saying to him, "Take heart; get up, he is calling you." So throwing off his cloak, he sprang up and came to Jesus. Then Jesus said to him, "What do you want me to do for you?" The blind man said to him, "My teacher, let me see again." Jesus said to him, "Go; your faith has made you well." Immediately he regained his sight and followed him on the way. (Mark 10:46–52)

Imagine walking dusty roads alongside Jesus during biblical times. What would you see? How would you feel? What smells would waft in the air? Would the dust between your toes irritate? Where would you be among the jostling crowds?

We easily imprint our twenty-first century lives upon first-century Gospel stories. One way to meet Jesus in the stories of his life is to engage our senses—sight, sound, touch, taste, and smell—imagine we are a part of the Gospel story. How is the Jesus who walked this earth beckoning you to meet him in your life today?

Reflect

Rest in silence and pray for the grace to meet Jesus in scripture. Slowly read the story of Bartimaeus twice. As you read, imagine the scene, pay keen attention to who is mentioned and where you find yourself located as events unfold. Then, close your eyes and replay the scene again. Note any sights, smells, feelings that you have. Encounter Jesus gazing at you and asking, "What do you want me to do for you?" Linger here and then write about your experience. Give thanks.

This exercise may be done alone or in small groups. The "Pray as You Go" app has audio contemplative scripture exercises. Ignatian spirituality offers another resource: www.ignatianspirituality.com/ignatian-prayer/the-spiritual-exercises/pray-with-your-imagination.

All Shall Be Well

Then Jesus told them a parable about their need to pray always and not to lose heart. (Luke 18:1)

One summer I was with the youth staff at Camp McDowell. They strung prayer beads in unique ways known best to the young. The tactile process partnered with repetitive prayer enhanced our ability to drop away from daily distractions, lifting our hearts to God. We prayed with our beads as we closed our time together. Reflecting upon our time, many expressed gratitude for experiencing that which can be illusive—peace. Later in the summer, when I spoke with the staff, some mentioned their prayer beads as a source of strength when facing cranky kids, loneliness from home, or questioning their faith.

Occasionally sleep alludes me. Following the wisdom of another, I have chosen to take this time as an invitation from God for time together and go into our spare bedroom to pray. Raised Catholic, I remember praying the rosary with my parents and seven siblings. I liked how it felt to slip the pretty pink beads through my fingers as we chanted our prayers together. Later, when I was studying Tibetan Buddhism, it was Mala beads sliding through those same fingers chanting, "Om Mani Padme Hum." Now that I have returned to my Christian roots, I find solace in the Anglican rosary. Frequently, it is the blue prayer beads from a cherished boy that I reach for in the middle of the night. Afterward, I am often able to drop back into peaceful sleep. Always I am closer to God.

Reflect

King of Peace Episcopal Church in Kingsland, Georgia, offers prayers and instructions for praying with beads.[16] Many local Episcopal bookstores carry Anglican prayer beads or they can be purchased online.

Even if you do not currently have beads, you may pray this prayer inspired by Dame Julian of Norwich.

Pray:

God of your goodness, give me yourself,
For you are enough to me.
And I can ask for nothing less that is to
your glory. And if I ask for anything less,
I shall still be in want, for only in you have
I all.

---

16. "Anglican Prayer Beads: A Form of Meditative Prayer," King of Peace, accessed December 3, 2018 www.kingofpeace.org/prayerbeads .htm.

Then repeat seven times:

All shall be well, and all shall be well,
And all manner of things shall be well.

Repeat this cycle four times and conclude with the Lord's Prayer.

Worship

DAY 25

Pray

Bless

Learn

Go

Turn

Rest

Belonging

But to all we received him, who believed in his name, he gave power to become children of God, who were born, not of blood or of the will of the flesh or of the will of man, but of God. (John 1:12–13)

The first two baptisms I performed were on the same day—a beautiful little girl adopted from China and an active five-year-old boy in foster care. "Derrick has lived with us for two years already and wants to be baptized," his foster mother told me. "Will you help us?"

The day I poured holy water on those dear children, it was not lost on the congregation how much longing and loving had been poured into them already. Making the sign of the cross with my oil-soaked thumb on their foreheads, I claimed each was, "Sealed by the Holy Spirit in baptism and marked as Christ's own *forever.*" Long ago claimed into the hearts of so many, we celebrated their adoption into God's family. Frequently squirmy children sat mesmerized around the baptismal font, surrounding their newest spiritual siblings. Sure, there was no mistaking that neither child carried a single biological gene from his or her parents; however there was no mistaking both children carried an abundance of love imprinted on their souls.

When St. Athanasius said, "For the Son of God became man so that we might become God,"[17] he was referring to *theosis*—growing in sanctification, growing in holiness. "We are imprinted with God's image at birth," said the Rt. Rev. Frank Griswold. "Likeness is what we are growing toward."[18] *Theosis* is not a private matter; it is done in and for community—those living and the communion of saints.

We are a sacramental people, sanctified as we participate in the sacramental life of the Church. We mark time and our spiritual lives in community.

Two years later, I was invited to witness Derrick's long-awaited adoption—no longer would he be a foster child, he would claim the name of the people who had shown him what God's love looks like. After the judge interviewed Derrick and his parents, she proclaimed the adoption final. Then, she invited Derrick to come up to her bench, stand on her chair, and proclaim while peering down upon all of us in the courtroom, his complete, new legal name. "I am Derrick. . . ." Cheers and tears erupted. Sealed by the Holy Spirit in baptism, marked as Christ's and his parents' own *forever.*

---

17. St. Athanasius in his work *On the Incarnation.*

18. The Most Reverend Frank Griswold speaking during his class "Anglican Spirituality" at Virginia Theological Seminary on February 23, 2013.

Reflect

How does community help or hinder your growing in union with Christ?

How can you strengthen the life of your faith community?

Inner Nature

So we do not lose heart. Even though our outer nature is wasting away, our inner nature is being renewed day by day. (2 Cor. 4:16)

Dr. Tully crawled into my heart and took up residence. It wasn't just those sparkling blue eyes, or his, at times, bawdy sense of humor, it was something unseen in the essence of the man. The last time we were together, he held my hand. I had been here before, by the bedside of someone who knows what is true for all of us, but acute for them—our bodies don't last forever. Yet that wasn't what Dr. Tully wanted to talk about. He reminisced about family and fishing. He told jokes. Then he said, "I believe being a Christian made me a better doctor."

"In what way?" I asked.

"I hope I was kinder, more patient, more compassionate," he answered. Lying in his hospital bed, he told me his life had been a great journey and could not have been any better. "You're a grateful man," I said. "You have to be," he said. I thought, "Oh no, gratitude is a choice."

Outer nature declining; inner nature ascending.

That same week, I went to the "Twelve Tribes Vacation Bible School," a joy-filled environment for children to learn about Jesus. The pavilion was christened by children's laughter. When Dr. Tully told me, "I think being a Christian made me a better doctor," he reminded me why we come together as a faith community.

Those bandana-covered children will grow up one day. We owe it to God, to them, and to the world, to give them a chance to know Jesus. We are all ordained by our baptism. We need more priestly doctors, priestly lawyers, priestly teachers, and priestly politicians. Those precious ones need to know they belong to and are loved by us and by God.

Reflect

One of the ways we "bless" is to be present with those who are closest to us; embodying Jesus' teachings as best we can. Who are you regularly present with?

Who has taught you how to live a Jesus-centered life?

Who have you taught?

It's All God's Vineyard

No one after lighting a lamp puts it under the bushel basket, but on the lampstand, and it gives light to all in the house. (Matt. 5:15)

For many of us choosing to follow in the Way of Love, the question is not do we desire to faithfully serve God, but, how shall we serve? There are as many ways to be a disciple as there are people. For some of us, it is freeing to have choices. For others, it is overwhelming. Pressure presses on good people discerning movement in the "right" direction. When the steps forward include experiencing a peace which surpasses all understanding, that is grace. When peace is absent, it is disquieting.

Many years ago, my husband, Malcolm, agreed to do a second-year chaplain residency with Dr. Wayne Oates, the psychologist and religious educator who coined the word "workaholic." A couple of months later, Malcolm was offered a dream job as a minister of pastoral care at a church he loved. His angst was great over these two wonderful choices. Finally, he approached Dr. Oates to decide what he should do. "What do you want to do?" Oates asked. "I want to follow God's will." To which the pastoral care sage replied, "I'm not sure God cares, Malcolm, as long as you're working in God's vineyard." After a pause Oates added, "And, by the way, it's all God's vineyard."

At the core of our desire to please God is the intention to be of service; and from that service to make meaning of our lives. Yes, specific choices are important in the particulars of how our lives unfold. And the movement of lifting our heart to God to be of service is the genesis of being that which we desire—a living sacrifice to God. If we remind ourselves each day of this intention, we will find we have been faithful tenders of the vineyard in which we have been planted. Acute awareness of the "Sacrament of the Present Moment"[19] opens our eyes to see the presence of Christ in all moments.

Reflect

Create a prayer that represents your desire to serve God and follow Jesus.

Sometimes we find ourselves at a time of deep discernment. A spiritual director can be an excellent sounding board. Two outstanding resources for times for those times are Listening Hearts: http://listeninghearts.org and Ignatian spirituality: www.ignatianspirituality.com/making-good-decisions/discernment-of-spirits.

---

19. This is the title of the first of three texts written by Jesuit priest Jean-Pierre de Caussade (1675–1751).

Pray · Worship · Bless · Learn · Go · Turn · Rest

Still Voices in the Storm

He said, "Go out and stand on the mountain before the Lord, for the Lord is about to pass by." Now there was a great wind, so strong that it was splitting mountains and breaking rocks in pieces before the Lord, but the Lord was not in the wind; and after the wind an earthquake, but the Lord was not in the earthquake; and after the earthquake a fire, but the Lord was not in the fire; and after the fire a sound of sheer silence. (1 Kings 19:11–12)

When Hurricane Irma hit Tortola in September 2017, 200 mph winds upended homes and lives. Six months after the storm, I visited Tortola to facilitate a retreat. Twisted remnants of metal and flattened homes dotted the island. Dust filled the air, trash can liners served as makeshift car windows; families had been thrown together in small spaces and children were sent far away for school.

Saturday morning we sat in a circle in the parish hall, boxes of hurricane provisions stacked in the corner. A young man strummed a familiar hymn and weary voices soared praise to on high. Then we chanted:

Be still and know that I am God
Be still and know that I am
Be still and know
Be still
Be

We rested in silence. Eyes closed, I invited them to let their souls catch up to them. Sighs too deep for words filled the space. Soon after, they told stories of loss and hope, fear and resilience. Somehow coming together in this soaked-in-prayer space, faces softened, laughter lit the room. Hardships were still ahead, but a breather from the intensity of recovery gave strength to rebuild.

Ronald Rolheiser offers the Upper Room as an image to guide us when we are lost and not sure what next to do. "Pentecost did not happen to a solitary man or woman. . . . It happened to a group of men and women at a church meeting . . . where men and women, frightened for their future, were huddled in fear, confusion, and uncertainty, but were gathered in faith and fidelity despite their fears."[20]

Gathering as a people of faith is an important part of our sabbath taking. Bible studies, men's breakfasts, retreats, and other ways of coming together can help to strengthen our connection to God. And here on Tortola amid the destruction, at lunch a woman explained

---

20. Rolheiser, *Sacred Fire*, 131.

that there were flowers blooming on the island that had not bloomed there in decades. Seeds stirred up from the storms, or carried by the winds from surrounding islands, bore fruit once more.

We are strengthened in the coming together—spirits stronger as we faithfully trust that the spark will return and offering witness to the new signs that we see. All of our resurrections bear the marks of the cross.

Reflect

What groups do you participate in that help to renew your faith? If you have one or more, give thanks.

If this is an area lacking in your life, how might you connect with others in the spirit of rest and renewal?

Be Who You Are

We have gifts that differ according to the grace given to us: prophecy, in proportion to faith; ministry, in ministering; the teacher, in teaching; the exhorter, in exhortation; the giver, in generosity; the leader, in diligence; the compassionate, in cheerfulness. (Rom. 12:6–8)

Recently, I was one of a multiwoman team facilitating a women's retreat. One woman held all of the important logistical details and gracefully taught yoga. Another organized art supplies, cheerfully encouraging the reticent to try an art project. Another gently led centering prayer and labyrinth walks. And another quietly created sacred space, placing bud vases and lighting candles while no one was looking.

Each of us shared one of the gifts we love to share, this time as a team together. In the past, when I have been a staff of one—holding all of the details—I would sometimes become anxious. Knowing I need only focus on the component I most love—providing spiritual enrichment material and facilitating deeper connections—I was free to gratefully provide what I had to offer. And my soul rejoiced. Each of us was given space to offer what brought us satisfaction.

Tranquil walks in the woods and lingering conversations beckoned us to an unhurried pace. At the retreat we pondered together that which we hold most dear. Strangers became friends. God's presence made known in silence, laughter, music, and prayer. Like a colorful tapestry woven together with unique threads, the retreat culminated in a glorious experience for leaders and participants alike—because each person contributed in her unique, important way.

Bishop Curry emboldens each of us to "turn my life like a flower turning toward the sun; to turn my life in the direction of God's love; in the direction of Jesus."[21] One of the ways we do this is to pay attention to those gifts we love to share and trust that God planted the seed. When we nurture those seeds, God's love shines on and grows them. Others are graced by the beauty of the flowers they become. Each of us have things we love to do. St. Francis de Sales wrote, "Be who you are and be that well."[22]

---

21. Curry, Way of Love, https://www.episcopalchurch.org/explore-way-love.

22. Saint Francis de Sales, *Introduction to the Devout Life* (St. Louis: Aeterna Press, 2015), 60.

Reflect

What brings you great joy? Where does your soul sing? What is it that you find yourself doing and getting lost in the process?

How can you take time to make this activity a regular part of your life? How might you share it with others for the benefit of something greater than yourself?

Watch this eight-minute video about a man who is described by the Collegeville Institute in this way: "As a new immigrant in New York City, Francois found himself in crisis, wondering what God wanted from him. Discover how a career he never expected brought him deep joy."

*https://collegevilleinstitute.org/vocation-projects/
resources-for-congregations/lives-explored/*

Follow Me

As he walked by the Sea of Galilee, he saw two brothers, Simon, who is called Peter, and Andrew his brother, casting a net into the lake—for they were fishermen. And he said to them, "Follow me, and I will make you fish for people." Immediately they left their nets and followed him. As he went from there, he saw two other brothers, James son of Zebedee and his brother John, in the boat with their father Zebedee, mending their nets, and he called them. Immediately they left the boat and their father, and followed him. (Matt. 4:18–22)

As we enter our fifth week of intentionally taking time with God each day, I hope the Spirit is awakening fresh encounters with Jesus. If you are finding it challenging to stay grounded in the daily practice, I encourage you to take heart and trust that God is growing you. There is power in our following through with commitments; it is also wise to be gentle with ourselves when we fall short, simply returning our hearts to God.

Esther de Waal writes, "It is our obedience which proves that we have been paying close attention. That word 'obedience' is derived from the Latin *oboedire*, which shares its root from *audire*, to hear. So to obey really means to hear and then act upon what we have heard, or, in other words, to see that the listening achieves its aim."[23]

Below is an exercise that invites encounter with scripture as well as a response to follow God's invitation toward greater love.

Reflect

Consent to God's presence and action within while you pray with the above scripture from the Gospel of Matthew.

Slowly read this passage aloud and ask: How does this speak to what is happening in the world today?

Read the passage aloud a second time, asking: What guidance is the Holy Spirit offering for my community/family/church through this story?

---

23. De Waal, *Seeking God,* 43.

Read the passage aloud a third time. Seek the guidance of the Holy Spirit and ask: How does this encounter with scripture speak to me in my life today? Allow a gracious space of time to ponder this question and write your response.

Finally, ask: What is Jesus calling me to do in response to this scripture? Pray for the grace and courage to respond, to obey.

A Rare Treasure

"Be still, and know that I am God!" (Ps. 46:10)

One obstacle to maturing in faith is distractions. Addiction to technology is overwhelming. Insatiable desires for information and affirmation devour precious hours. The mind churns and burns for more and more as the soul yearns for less and less. Silence is a rare treasure. This is not to say that silence is always comforting. One of the reasons we avoid silence is because when we eliminate noise we think that we can control, we are infused with thoughts and feelings that seem out of control. Like a classroom of toddlers at nap time, in the silence, unclaimed hurts vie for attention; unresolved problems seek solutions; untended tasks clamor as gongs.

John of the Cross writes, "God's first language is silence."[24] Thomas Keating adds, "Everything else is a poor

---

24. As quoted in William Johnston and Huston Smith, *The Cloud of Unknowing and the Book of Privy Counseling* (New York: Doubleday, 1996), 121.

translation. In order to hear that language, we must learn to be still and to rest in God."[25]

Prayer is God's activity in us. At the heart of prayer is love—God's love for us and our love for God. Just as one diamond can only be cut by another, prayer refines us— our indwelling spirit refined by the Holy Spirit. "Prayer is not a request for God's favours. Genuine prayer is based on recognizing the origin of all that exists and opening ourselves to it. In prayer we acknowledge God as the supreme source from which flows all strength, all goodness, all existence."[26]

We can trust that our time in silence with God will cultivate an awareness beyond our own spiritual growth and a desire to be of service. First, and regularly, we must be still and know that God is God.

---

25. Thomas Keating, *Invitation to Love: The Way of Christian Contemplation,* 20th anniversary ed. (London: Bloomsbury, 2012), 105.

26. Cynthia Bourgeault speaking at St. Philip Anglican Church Oak Bay, Victoria, British Columbia, June 6, 1996, https://inaspaciousplace. wordpress.com/2014/12/27/cynthia-bourgeault-what-is-contemplative-prayer-1996/.

Reflect
Centering Prayer

Take twenty minutes for centering prayer.[27] You may wish to continue this practice on a daily basis.

1. Choose a sacred word as the symbol of your intention to consent to God's presence and action within.

2. Sitting comfortably and with eyes closed, settle briefly and silently introduce the sacred word as the symbol of your consent to God's presence and action within.

3. When engaged with your thoughts (including body sensations, feelings, images, and reflections), return ever-so-gently to the sacred word.

4. At the end of the prayer period, remain in silence with eyes closed for a couple of minutes.

You may wish to finish with the Lord's Prayer or a spontaneous prayer from your heart.

---

27. These instructions are courtesy of Contemplative Outreach, Ltd.: https://www.contemplativeoutreach.org/sites/default/files/private/method_cp_eng-2016-06_0.pdf.

Dining and Dashing

Create in me a clean heart, O God, and put a new and right spirit within me. (Ps. 51:10)

While in high school, a small group of us left a raucous party to grab Saturday night breakfast at a diner. Brazenly, one of us suggested we "dine and dash"—leave without paying our bill. Sneakily, we exited one at a time. The last person bolted out the door, jumping into my brown Ford Granada. Squeals from the tires matched squeals from our mouths. We were so cool.

Crawling into bed, a gnawing of guilt crept in. I was a waitress: I knew who would have to pay our bill. Eventually, I drifted off to sleep. Ironically, the next morning at church the sermon was focused on honesty and integrity. I don't remember the scripture; I don't remember Father Casey's exact words: I do remember the queasiness in my gut.

When we arrived home, I found an envelope and went to the drawer where I kept my cash. I put enough money in the envelope to pay our entire bill, plus a generous tip and wrote an unsigned note explaining what we did, and asking forgiveness. Then I drove the long two miles to the diner and approached the hostess, handing her the envelope with "manager" printed on the outside. Before anyone could open it, I ran to my car and left, never to return again.

I made lots of mistakes in high school, and many more since. This story reminds me of how growing up in a family of faith helps me to try to return again and again to being a better human being. One of the reasons we gather regularly for worship and Eucharist is to hear the stories from Jesus's life and be inspired to follow him. Being a part of a worshipping community helps us to turn away from selfish ways and turn toward God's love and mercy. We confess our shortcomings, receive absolution, and are invited at the Eucharist to "behold what you are. Become what you receive."[28]

Reflect

How does/has coming together for communal worship shape the way you live?

What seminal moments have you had that informed a need to return to Christ?

---

28. St. Augustine, Sermon 57, *On the Eucharist.* http://www.the diocese.net/Customer-Content/WWW/CMS/files/Council_2013/ council213_meditations.pdf

If you saw it as a step toward new life, who would you invite to join you at worship?

No Holding Back

"Truly I tell you, this poor widow has put in more than all those who are contributing to the treasury. For all of them have contributed out of their abundance; but she out of her poverty has put in everything she had, all she had to live on." (Mark 12:43–44)

When she was in the throes of raising three small children, Kim was approached by Mark, the deacon at Saint Luke's in Birmingham. He mentioned how Kim would be great at leading the parish's initiative to house homeless families for one week out of every quarter, were it not for how busy she was as a mom. Determined to prove him wrong, motivated to make life better for those who had no consistent place to lay their heads, Kim became the parish coordinator for the homeless initiative. That was twelve years ago; today she continues to do whatever it takes to provide comfort for the homeless.

Recently, Kim and her husband, David, offered to take three homeless teenagers who were staying at the church to a college football game—prime tickets for a primetime game. The extra tickets were a generous gift from Philip, a church member whose mother used to run the program before Kim. When it came time to go to the concession stand for dinner, one of the teenage boys said, "I only have $3.00." "You're our guests," Kim told him. "We will buy what you need." So the boy tucked the bills in his wallet and abandoned himself to the revelries of his first college football game.

As they were leaving the stadium, a woman near the gate held a sign "single mom three kids hungry." The group walked past her when the teenager called, "Y'all hold up." He ran back to the woman, dug in his wallet, and placed $3.00 in her basket. When he met up with Kim and David, he said, "I don't need that money anyway. It makes me feel good to contribute to society."

Our blessings have traction. When we choose to share the bounty that has been given us—however little or much, it ripples out like pebbles in a pond. Conversely, when we grip our goods, we block the energy of generosity.

Reflect

When you reflect upon your financial giving, would you say your palms are open or clenched?

How would you describe your stance to giving?

What person or cause or community could benefit from your generosity?

How have you planned for your generosity to continue beyond your life here on earth?

All Things Mend

"Do not be dismayed by the brokenness of the world. All things break. And all things can be mended. Not with time, as they say, but with intention. So go. Love intentionally, extravagantly, unconditionally. The broken world waits in darkness for the light that is you." —L. R. Knost[29]

Eleven candles rested on the table positioned at the temple's top step. A candle for each person killed on Shabbat at the Tree of Life Synagogue. Thousands gathered. We prayed. We sang. We cried. "Our sages tell us that one who saves a life has, in effect, saved an entire world," said Rabbi Moshe Rube, of Knesseth Israel. "And by contrast, those that take a life destroy a world. . . . My friends, we have lost worlds."

In honor of the eleven lost worlds, we were encouraged to build worlds and perform a combined 1,100 "mitzvot"—good deeds.[30] At the end of the prayer ser-

---

29. www.lrknost.com

30. One meaning of mitzvah is commandment. Rabbi Rube used mitzvah in the sense of doing a good deed, which is another meaning. Rabbi Moshe Rube, October 29, 2018, Temple Beth El, Birmingham, Alabama.

vice, the cantor turned her cell phone's flashlight on and began waiving her arm as she sang. We mirrored her action, phones twinkling on like stars in the evening sky.

Silently we marched to another temple blocks away. Hundreds of lights marked the way ahead. I turned around, light upon light upon light piercing the sky, piercing our grief-stricken hearts with hope; the dark horror of hate no match for the lights held by people of every race and religion.

Christians are a people of hope steeped in the resurrection of Jesus and in the tradition of our Jewish relatives. The book of Jeremiah contains oracles of hope.

> *You shall be my people, and I will be your God.*
> ***Again** you shall take your tambourines. . . .*
> ***Again** you shall plant vineyards.*
> (Jer. 30:22; 31:4–5)

Yes, we will return home restored, but with the wisdom borne from loss. For the Israelite people the physical loss of home in the Babylonian captivity. For us, the loss of our shared humanity and decency. We will return home, but we will bear the bruises of this bitter time of enmity. Like Jesus, we are to bring the fire of our love and cross safe boundaries and go to those who live differently, love differently, believe differently than we do. The world is rebuilt one mitzvah at a time.

Reflect

Where can you, with God's help, lovingly seek and serve Christ in someone who is different than you?

How can you advocate for peace and safety in your community?

Go. Love intentionally, extravagantly, unconditionally. The broken world waits in darkness for the light that is you.

Pray Worship Bless
Learn Go
Turn Rest

Transforming
the World One
Picture at a Time

*"God created this evolving universe because God is Love
and each of us is God's gift to the world. Our life purpose
is to make a difference in transforming that world."*
—Pierre Teilhard de Chardin[31]

Malcolm's hobby is nature photography. Recently, I
found him lying on the ground, camera to the sky, under
a maple tree flaming gold and orange leaves. When we
hike together, Malcolm often lags behind—captivated
by light shifting through trees, or an insect on a flower. I
used to resent this impediment to my burning maximum
calories on our jaunts through the woods. Now I appreciate how much joy it brings Malcolm to slow down and
see the world through the camera lens—colors bursting
vividly and insignificant creatures revealing epiphanies.
One of the ways Malcolm prays is to contemplate his
nature photography and then write encouraging say-

---

31. Pierre Teilhard de Chardin, *Toward the Future*, trans. René
Hague (New York: Harcourt Brace Jovanovich: 1975), xiii, 86–87.

ings to accompany his pictures. He posts them on social media, spreading the good news. Countless people are edified by his stunning photos and pithy proverbs.

Sometimes our creative outlets slow us down enough to appreciate the beauty that surrounds us; other times, they are lifelines propelling us forward when we feel we can't go on. I know of a mother whose tiny baby never left the hospital; her grief is incomprehensible. A heroic spark of life within the mother is thrusting her to keep living. She is creating photographic montages to honor her daughter. Other grieving parents have written stories and created quilts as tangible reminders of all that has been lost.

Incorporating a creative activity to sabbath time renews us to cocreate transformation with God. "Creative" is a loaded word; many of us falsely believe it does not apply to us. Among other things, we can be creative in the way that we love, cook, entertain children, and make our homes welcoming spaces. When we enjoy these pursuits without concern for outcome, we savor the process. This heightens our awareness and helps us experience Christ in the one place he will be revealed, the present moment. Creative sabbath time gives us the eyes to see and ears to hear how Christ is loving us forward.

Reflect

Where do you experience creative energy?

How do you regularly incorporate creativity in your life? How could you?

What impact do your creative outlets have on your taking rest? Is there a way you could claim creativity as sabbath?

Fist Bumps of Love

Finding no way to bring him in because of the crowd, they went up on the roof and let him down with his bed through the tiles into the middle of the crowd in front of Jesus. (Luke 5:19)

Gathering to pause and reflect at the end of a busy day, a women's group was discussing worship as a spiritual practice. Natalie said, "The best thing on earth is to watch when people come back from communion, approach Wilmer in his wheelchair, and fist bump him." Natalie was referring to a parishioner who had been a prominent businessman and beloved member of the community before suffering a severe stroke. Wilmer loved people— he would call clients on birthdays and stop to speak with shopkeepers when walking his laps at the mall. Now, he is confined to a wheelchair and verbal communication is nearly nonexistent. As often as possible, his wife, Carol, along with a caregiver bring Wilmer to church. They strategically place his wheelchair so he can participate in the service. Wilmer greets those who have just received the Bread and the Wine with his own form of communion— twinkling blue eyes, broad smile, and an arm raised for a fist bump. After all others have been served, a priest and a layperson approach Wilmer for fist bumps, hugs, and to give him communion.

Moved by Natalie's reflection, I called her to ask if I could share her story. She was happy to say, "It tears me up every time—despite where he is with his abilities and disabilities, Wilmer continues to communicate love in his openness. He doesn't care whether he knows you or not, whether you are rich or poor, you are going to get a smile and a fist bump. The natural response is to beam a smile and fist bump back. I have no doubt God is working through Wilmer and Carol—him loving everybody and anybody, and her selflessly caring for him. We are coming together to share bread, to be Jesus's disciples creating heaven on earth, and there is Wilmer being Jesus."

Natalie continued, "When I see the clergy come over to bring him communion, I think about the guy on the mat whose friends were so determined to get him close to Jesus. They brought him and Jesus paid attention. Here the clergy goes to meet him, all smiling, and seeming honored to give him communion, fist bump and all. When your eyes are open, it is amazing what you can see."

When I called Carol to ask if we could share this story, she was in the middle of making fudge for family. "Oh yes, please do," Carol said. "If it helps anyone, that would be great. You know, I didn't even know Natalie and she sent me a note about how much watching Wilmer means to her. That meant the world to me. People might feel those things, but she took the time to write." Seemingly unaware of her own Jesus-inspired service, Carol closed with, "I'm sorry, I've got to go stir my fudge."

Reflect

Where do you see Turn in this story?

Where do you see Learn in this story?

Pray?

Worship?

Bless?

Go?

Rest?

DAY 37

Building Your Trellis

"Out of the believer's heart shall flow rivers of living water." (John 7:38)

As I witness fall's glory—green leaves turning stunning oranges and reds—I am reminded of the impermanence and preciousness of life. How many turns of the seasons will each of us have? Awareness of the finitude of our days need not be morbid, but a reminder to savor each one. My hope is that having devoted time these past five weeks to strengthening or creating new practices that support living Jesus-centered lives, you have experienced a heightened awareness of the sacred in your days.

In support of continuing this following in the way of Jesus, we will spend the next few days creating a personal rule of life. As a reminder, a rule of life is like a trellis that guides us toward growing in our relationship with God, ourselves, others, and the created order. It helps us to prioritize who and what is most important in a world with multiple needs clamoring for our attention. Rather than being confining, a rule provides a framework. Patrick Henry writes, "[St.] Benedict says the Rule is *only a beginning* (73.2). The goal is the learning that one does all the time in this pattern of life. The trellis doesn't close off options. It multiplies them . . . expanding to grow with us."[32] Care is encouraged to avoid making the rule—and corresponding spiritual practices—goals or idols. The intention is to cocreate with God, who is growing us.

A rule of life is most helpful when it is simple, realistic, and flexible. The following exercises will address spiritual practices, core relationships, health, vocation, and creativity. The prompts on pages 112–114 are intended as a consolidation of all of the work you have done. Periodically reviewing our rule and creating a support system to encourage one another is also important.

Reflect

The first step for creating your personal rule of life will be to identify why having one is important to you.

How has being present with God in this intentional way impacted your experience of God? What do you desire moving forward in regard to growing in relationship with God?

---

32. Henry, *Benedict's Dharma*, 4.

What concerns do you have about creating a rule of life? What might you do to mitigate those concerns?

What benefits do you anticipate in having a trellis to provide a framework for your spiritual growth? How will relationships, health, and your life in Christ be impacted?

What relationships are most important to you? How will these relationships be enhanced by your having a rule of life?

Turn, Learn, Pray, and Worship

"I am the vine, you are the branches. Those who abide in me and I in them bear much fruit, because apart from me you can do nothing." (John 15:5)

God is with us at all times and in all places. Setting aside intentional time for prayer, study, and worship enhances our awareness of God's presence. Returning again and again to receive and then offer God's love, with God's help, we grow in love. Being specific about how we incorporate these practices in our daily lives, increases the likelihood we will actually follow through.

Reflect

How might you build pauses into your day to reflect on how the Spirit is working in your life?

How and when will you set aside time to pray and learn with God?

What prayer practices have most fed you either in the past, or during this Way of Love experience?

What will support your ongoing learning in studying scripture and Christian teachings?

What are you already doing and what do you desire to do in regard to gathering in communal worship? Why is worship important to you?

Bless, Go, and Rest

By contrast, the fruit of the Spirit is love, joy, peace, patience, kindness, generosity, faithfulness, gentleness, and self-control. (Gal. 5:22–23)

Regularly turning to Jesus and grounding ourselves in prayer, study, and worship, we cultivate hearts in sync with the heartbeat of God. As Christians we desire to grow in the fruit of the Spirit. Becoming more loving, joyful, peaceful, patient, kind, generous, faithful, gentle, and self-controlled is not a linear path. There are setbacks and frustrations; unexpected challenges temporarily derail us. Being rooted in Jesus-centered practices helps us to grow in the fruit of the Spirit even in, perhaps especially in, our darkest days. And when all is well, these practices serve as a ballast.

The rhythm of our days are patterned after the rhythm of Jesus' ways when we bless, go, and rest. Consider how you already are, or desire to incorporate these practices in your life.

Reflect

There are many ways to bless others; we have explored a few during these past forty days. Which ways of blessing resonate most with you? How can you remind yourself to be kind, to be thoughtful, and to bless on a regular basis?

How do you share your financial blessings with family, church, charitable organizations, or people in need? Is there somewhere you are withholding blessing?

Within the realm of your vocation(s) and everyday life, how do others experience the love of Christ through you?

What boundaries have you crossed in these past few weeks? Where do you desire to create or deepen a relationship with a person or others who are different than you?

What pattern of rest is incorporated in your week? If you already intentionally take sabbath time, give thanks and reaffirm your commitment to it. If not, how might you incorporate sabbath from work, technology, busyness?

What activities bring you joy that you can assimilate into your life? What renews your spirit?

What ways do you commit to care for your body? How often and when will you exercise? Are there food, drink, or substance use habits that hinder your health? How will you avoid them?

DAY 40

A Support System

For the letter kills, but the Spirit gives life. (2 Cor. 3:6)

"There is no salvation through willpower alone. . . . What we need during our adult years is something that can empower us beyond our own strength, a fire beyond our own, a baptism into grace and community."[33] The Christian life has always been lived out in community.

In the Celtic tradition the term *anam cara* is translated as "soul friend." My friend Angie and I meet most Sundays for lunch—hallowed space on our cluttered calendars. After years of friendship, we have settled into the soft and at times challenging place, what Irish poet and priest John O'Donohue calls "home." When I am worried, Angie listens. Dark or selfish thoughts lose their power under the light of her candid gaze. Wild ideas brought to the table may be discarded before the waiter arrives, but at least they will have had their audience. I am fortunate to have a trusted soul friend with whom to wonder, "Where is the Spirit dancing today?" I am grateful she

---

33. Rolheiser, *Sacred Fire*, 130.

calls me out when I am fooling myself or copping out on that which I hold most dear.

My spiritual director, Karen, listens prayerfully to all aspects of my life. She helps me look for God in everything and offers guidance on practices that can support faithfulness. I also meet regularly with a centering prayer group. I am grateful for these support systems that are vital for me to live closer to my values.

Everyone needs at least one soul friend. Describing this kind of relationship, O'Donohue writes, "In this love, you are understood as you are without mask or pretension. The superficial and functional lies and half-truths of social acquaintance fall away, you can be as you really are. Love allows understanding to dawn, and understanding is precious. Where you are understood, you are at home."[34]

Reflect

Who supports your living a Jesus-centered life? What person, or group of people, would you like to meet with regularly to check in on how you are living according to your values?

---

34. John O'Donohue, *Anam Cara* (New York: Harper Collins, 1997), 14.

It can be challenging to identify a friend or family member to support you in this way. Remember that you are not alone. Pray for the strength to seek and the grace to find a group or person in whom you can trust. If you are part of a church, perhaps you can approach the clergy for a small group to join. Is there a Bible study or centering prayer group nearby? You may go to www.sdiworld.org to search for a spiritual director.

Epilogue

Let the same mind be in you that was in Christ Jesus.
(Phil. 2:5)

This forty-day pilgrimage of practicing the way of love has reached its completion. But it is not the end. My hope is that your faithfulness has been fruitful and that at least some of what you desired when you embarked on this pilgrimage has been fulfilled. Also, that you are affirmed in practices you had already incorporated in your daily life and that new ones have called to you.

Below are questions to assist you in developing a personalized rule of life. This is a culmination of the many questions you have already considered and is intended as a resource for you to periodically return. If this list is overwhelming, prayerfully choose one area of focus and build from there. Just as a slight turn in the rudder of a ship creates momentum to change course, so too can one small turn in the direction you desire to go be beneficial. Remember to keep your rule as simple, achievable, and flexible as possible within the context of your current stage of life.

Reflect

How will you create pauses in your day to turn toward God?

When will you take time for prayer? What practices will ground your prayer life?

How will you on a daily or weekly basis continue to grow in your knowledge and love of God through scripture and Christian teachings? Is there a group you already belong to, or one that you could join, that will support your learning?

When and where will you worship?

How will you bless God and others with your time, gifts, talents, and financial resources? What percentage of your income or financial amount will you joyfully give to share your blessings?

Where will you cross boundaries to develop new or deepen current relationships? Where will you participate in God's dream for beloved community?

What relationships are most important to you? How will you make them a priority in your daily life?

How will you care for your physical health? What habits will you continue or adopt? What habits will you discontinue?

How will you create boundaries around technology in your life?

What excites you about sabbath time? How can you make time for creativity, rest, and play? When will you take time for sabbath—daily? weekly?

A rule is meant to serve humans and not the other way around; it is not to become an idol, simply a trellis for growth. Living a rule of life sharpens our eyes to see and ears to hear Jesus calling us toward deeper and deeper love. Therefore, we are wise to avoid becoming legalistic or rigid about our rules. Be gentle with yourself. Accountability to another, or a group, is helpful to living in accordance with your rule.

Who will you partner with for mutual support in living in accordance with your rule?

How often will you review and adapt your rule?

Thank you for spending these past forty days in pondering the way of love. I pray God's peace and blessings in your life. As you follow Jesus in the way of love, may you grow in love, joy, peace, patience, kindness, generosity, faithfulness, gentleness, and self-control (Gal. 5:22–23). Amen.

Resources for Living the Way of Love

Facilitator's Guide

A facilitator's guide has been developed for using this book in small groups over a period of eight weeks. The group is designed to meet once a week in which participants will focus on one practice per week while supporting one another in following each of the practices. It is available to download and duplicate at www.churchpublishing .org/livingthewayoflove.

Worship

The Episcopal Church's website offers a church locator in which you can find an Episcopal church near you: www .episcopalchurch.org/find-a-church.

Pray

Many of the following websites are also available as apps so you can keep your prayer practice at the tip of your finger at any time of day or night.

Book of Common Prayer online: https://bcponline.org

Daily Prayer with The Mission of St. Clare: www
.missionstclare.com/english

Centering Prayer: www.contemplativeoutreach.org

The Episcopal Church: www.episcopalchurch.org/
way-of-love/pray

The Examen Prayer Card: www.ignatianspirituality
.com/19076/examen-prayer-card

Forward Day by Day: https://prayer.forwardmovement
.org

Pray as You Go: www.pray-as-you-go.org

Rule of Life

Companions on the Way (Northumbrian Community)
Rule of Life: http://companionsontheway.org/about/
new-monasticism/rule-of-life/

The Order of the Daughters of the King: www.dok
national.org/page/RuleofLife

The Rule of the Society of St. John the Evangelist:
www.ssje.org/worship/rule-of-life-resources

Labyrinths

Labyrinth Locator: https://labyrinthlocator.com

The Labyrinth Society: https://labyrinthsociety.org

Veriditas: www.veriditas.org

Spiritual Directors and Spiritual Director Training Programs

Haden Institute: www.hadeninstitute.com
Metagem Institute: http://metageminstitute.org
Shalem Institute: https://shalem.org
Spiritual Directors International: www.sdiworld.org/
    find-a-spiritual-director

Religious Orders and Faith Communities

These communities often offer retreats (locations noted) and have spiritual directors available. Their websites also offer daily prayer resources, many of which are available as apps.

Anamchara Fellowship (Celtic) (Newark, Delaware):
    www.anamcharafellowship.org
The Brotherhood of Saint Gregory (Gregorian): https://
    gregorians.org
The Community of Celebration (modified Benedictine)
    (Aliquippa, Pennsylvania): www.communityof
    celebration.com
Community of the Gospel (Waupaca, Wisconsin):
    www.communityofthegospel.org
The Community of the Holy Spirit (St. Hilda's House,
    New York City; Melrose Convent, Brewster, New
    York): www.chssisters.org

Community of Saint Francis (Franciscan) (San Francisco, California): www.communitystfrancis.org

The Community of St. John the Baptist (Mendham, New Jersey): www.csjb.org

The Companions of St. Luke (Benedictine): www.companions-osb.org

Community of St. Mary (Benedictine) (Sewanee, Tennessee): http://stmary-conventsewanee.org

Community of the Transfiguration (Cincinnati, Ohio): www.ctsisters.org

The Little Sisters of St. Clare (Franciscan) (western Washington State): www.stclarelittlesisters.org

Order of the Holy Cross (Benedictine) (West Park, New York): https://holycrossmonastery.com

The Order of Julian of Norwich (White Lake, Wisconsin): www.orderofjulian.org

Order of Saint Helena (North Augusta, South Carolina): www.osh.org

The Rivendell Community (Memphis, Tennessee; Kansas City, Missouri; Houston, Texas; St. Louis, Missouri)

Sacred Heart Monastery (Benedictine) (Cullman, Alabama): www.shmon.org

Saint Gregory's Abbey (Benedictine) (Three Rivers, Michigan): www.saintgregorysthreerivers.org

Saint Mary's Sewanee: The Ayres Center for Spiritual Development (Sewanee, Tennessee): www.stmaryssewanee.org

Sisters of St. Anne Bethany (Arlington, Massachusetts): www.osa-bethany.org

Sisters of Saint Anne Chicago (Chicago, Illinois): www.sistersofstannechicago.org

The Sisters of Saint Gregory (Mechanicsburg, Pennsylvania): www.sistersofsaintgregory.org

Society of Saint Francis (Franciscan) (San Francisco, California): www.ssfamericas.org

Society of Saint John the Evangelists (Cambridge, Massachusetts): www.ssje.org

Society of St. Margaret (Duxbury, Massachusetts): http://societyofstmargaret.org

The Third Order of the Society of St. Francis (Franciscan) (New York City; Philadelphia; Middle Tennessee): http://tssf.org

Acknowledgments

Unbeknownst to me at the time, I began writing this book in the spring, months before the "Way of Love" became a call to the Episcopal Church from Presiding Bishop Curry at the 79th General Convention. Thanks to the generosity of Saint Luke's Episcopal Church in Birmingham, Alabama, I secluded myself in a cabin to write for a week. Carol Henderson, my writing coach, guided me during that week and I reconnected with my love of writing. I am grateful to Carol for kindling the flame.

Time with the women who participated in the Way of Love circles provided the impetus to write this book. Your hearts are imprinted here. My life is richer because of you. Thank you. It is a gift to share ministry with generous and encouraging colleagues. I am appreciative of the Reverends Rich Webster, Rebecca Debow, Cameron Nations, Mark Lagory, and Katy Smith, who have shouldered some of my pastoral and preaching responsibilities so that I could finish this project.

I am grateful to the entire Saint Luke's family—staff and parishioners. Your care for one another and the greater community is inspiring. Your support and acceptance of Malcolm and me makes Birmingham home.

I give thanks for all of the congregations who have patiently and lovingly helped to shape my becoming a priest—Grace in Cullman, Alabama; Saint Alban's in Washington, DC; Holy Spirit in Alabaster, Alabama; and of course, Saint Luke's. My bishop, the Right Reverend Kee Sloan, is a generous encourager and reminds me that writing is essential to my ministry—for that I give thanks.

As I was fleshing out these initial reflections, Ann Johnson, Sandy Porter, and Angie Wright served as editors and exuberant encouragers. Along with Kathy Graham, they spurred me to compile them into a book. This was made possible by the willingness of Sharon Ely Pearson, my editor at Church Publishing Incorporated, to consider this devotional, and in full disclosure, work at breakneck speed, to make it available in time for Lent 2019. Sharon has made the process joy-filled and smooth. I am grateful to Kelly Warsak, who oversaw this book through the production process, and the entire Church Publishing team for rallying behind *Living the Way of Love.*

Inspiration for this book came from the insightful work of the Most Reverend Michael Curry and all who deemed it critical that we return to the basics in following Jesus, to the Way of Love. I give thanks for their creating such a platform for these reflections.

The family and friends of priests and writers are accustomed to vacant seats at important meals, unexpected absences because of a pastoral emergency, or the impulse of a creative idea. If your loved one is both, it can require a double-dose of sacrificial love. I am surrounded by the most wonderful people. Thank you to my cherished friends who provide laughter and comfort and joy.

I am especially grateful to and for my family. My parents, Margaret Mary and Dave Krohn, and my siblings Kathy, Liz, Dave, Mike, Anne, Patrick, and Maureen taught me about God, negotiating life, gratitude, and love. Thank you to the many in-laws who have made our family richer. I treasure the honor as a parent of watching my children, Brendan and Kiki, become kind, passionate, and amazing adults. We have fun. We humans have yet to create a language expansive enough to describe how much I love you. And to my beloved Malcolm: the axis of my world shifted when you entered in. It is you who brought me back to Christ and always you who loves me home. I often say, "I wish everyone had a Malcolm." I give thanks that I do.

CPSIA information can be obtained
at www.ICGtesting.com
Printed in the USA
LVHW040729040320
648908LV00005B/5

9 781640 652309